ADVENTURES IN PARADISE
Missionary Memoirs from Papua New Guinea

by
Esther Henry

*With special thanks to
- Brian Henry -

My wonderful husband,
whose inspiration and support for
me has never wavered.*

**Copyright © 2002-2012
Esther Henry**

All rights reserved. No part of this book may be reproduced in any form, except for the inclusion of brief quotations in a review, without written permission from the author.

Photography and layout by Esther Henry.
All photographs contained in this book are copyrighted © Esther Henry.

This volume is dedicated to my parents:

James & June McCoy.
They taught me what it was like to love the Lord with all my heart and instilled in me a desire to do His will. For their undying love and belief in me, I dedicate this book to them.

* * * *

Special mention should be made of:

Rev. & Mrs. Richard Carver Founders of the work in PNG May God continue to bless your endeavors wherever He may lead you! Thank you for being sensitive to the Lord.

TABLE OF CONTENTS:

Foreword
Introduction
Prologue
Chapter 1:   The Way It Was

Chapter 2:   A Letter to Mom
Chapter 3:   Front Porch Musings

Chapter 4:   Bon Apetite !

Chapter 5:   Village Life

Chapter 6:   Culture Shock! – Short Term

Chapter 7:   Culture Shock! – Long Term

Chapter 8:   Bible School

Chapter 9:   Setbacks (*by Brian Henry*)

Chapter 10: Miracles Never Cease

Chapter 11: When the Spirit Moves

Recipes

Order Information

This photo is perhaps the most popular photo we've taken to date. It has been featured in numerous church periodicals, including the Pentecostal Herald. Photo is of Brian standing with some Asaro Mudmen.

Circa 1996

FOREWORD

When Brian and Esther were students in our classes at Christian Life College, we found they were optimistic, enthusiastic, dependable, practical, honest, sincere, and both had a great sense of humor. Before they went to Papua New Guinea, they met Albert Gigmai, a student from there, who spoke "Pidgin" with them. They, in turn, would excitedly share the phrases with us along with their comment, "Isn't that a great way to say that!"

While reading *Adventures in Paradise*, you'll discover they are also courageous. We found their book fascinating and easy to read. We didn't put it down until we had finished the whole thing! Stories like the miracle of the robe are believable because we know Brian and Esther are honest. They "tell it like it is" including disappointments and discouragement, as well as exciting victories and hilarious times.

We can recommend *Adventures in Paradise* as a great read for anyone.

Arlo and Jane Moehlenpah

INTRODUCTION

The nation of Papua New Guinea [PNG] is located 100 miles off the northern coast of Australia in the South Pacific, and shares an island with Indonesia. The town where we reside, *Goroka*, is located in the mountains at an elevation of 5,500 ft above sea level. Although our town is located only 6° south of the Equator, the temperature is near perfect year-round because of its higher elevation. The temperatures will range between the high 50's to low 60's at night, to between 75° to 80° during the day. There are six months of rain, and six months of shine (wet and dry). Those are the only two seasons we have.

The highlanders that we live and work among were first discovered in 1930. As you can imagine, with only 72 years as a "discovered" people, many in the outlying villages are still living in the Stone Age. The last tribe was only discovered in 1986, and was a mere 50 kilometers from our largest highland town, Mt. Hagen! From reports we've heard, there are still tribes and villages that are suspected of existing, but never officially discovered by government officials.

They call Papua New Guinea the *Land of the Unexpected*. How true it is! Whether driving along the road or living daily life, you never know what's just around the corner. At the compiling and editing of the stories for this book, I was amused at how we reacted to some of the things experienced when we first came to Papua New Guinea. Everything was so very new to us. Things that were such a thrill then, are now just a part of our every day life. As you read this book you will take the journey with us from the very beginning.

As I reminisce over the years of experiences, the newness of it all, the deep culture shock, the adjustments, the ingraining of ourselves into "culture", the trials and then the triumphs, I am reminded once again of how very personal and real our Heavenly Father is! He alone has been the sole comfort in times of loneliness and sickness. He alone has protected us through everything and given us victories we could never claim as our own.

Come along with us in our exciting adventures in Papua New Guinea, *Land of the Unexpected*. May you enjoy the journey!

PROLOGUE

It all began as a child. Being raised in a pastor's home, I knew about the ministry, and my goals even then, included someday becoming a missionary. I would scour through *National Geographic* magazines, see all the different faces and customs of the world, and think to myself, "Someday I'm going to be a missionary to these people."

It was never an issue of doubt. I knew that God would someday call me to serve Him in the ministry. My wonderful parents, James and June McCoy (Cedar Rapids, IA), never gave up on me, even in the midst of my tumultuous teen years. By the age of 19, I had made up my mind to serve the Lord no matter what, and headed off to Bible College.

It was at Bible College in Stockton, CA where I met my husband, Brian Henry. In one of the very first conversations that we can recall, he asked me how I felt about missions. We spent the next 3½ hours sharing with each other our burden. We were hooked! That was all it took, and seven months later we tied the knot.

After both of us finished our years at Christian Life College and graduated, we moved to Tacoma, WA to work full time as administrators at the Tacoma UPC, pastored by Rev. Frank R.

LaCrosse. We were happy there, yet always in the back of our minds was this burning desire to go to the mission field. We did not have a particular place in mind but knew without a doubt the Lord was calling us. In 1985, while in prayer, the Lord gave Brian a burden for "the islands of the sea." We knew not where this path would take us, but knew it would be an island somewhere in the world. We just patiently waited for the Lord to open the doors.

In 1993 we took the long drive back to Stockton to be in a friend's wedding. While we were there, Daryl Rash, former missionary and local Missions Director for Christian Life Center, invited us into his office. The Lord had been dealing with him about asking us to go to the Marshall Islands to help them with the school there. We were so overwhelmed that we could not sleep that night. At 2:00 AM, I gave up trying to sleep and went to our host's living room and began to intercede before God. Was this the time? Was this the right thing to do? When it was all said and done, and before we even left Stockton to go back home to Tacoma, we both knew God was telling us it was time to go.

It took us a good three months of prayer and consecration before we were ready to broach the subject with our pastor. When we finally spoke to him about it, the Lord again showed us we were in His will. Bro. LaCrosse told us that he and his wife had just been talking about our ministry the previous night, and how they felt we needed to "spread our wings." They would back us up 100%, and they knew this was the Lord. We were thankful for yet another confirmation.

As the months of preparation passed, we had resigned from our position at the Tacoma UPC, and had trained our replacement. Things were in full swing now and there was no going back! Then one fateful day a call came from Daryl Rash. He apologized that the school in the Marshall Islands was not ready at this time, but he had just returned from Papua New Guinea (where in the world was *that?*) and they needed a school desperately. Would we be willing to go there instead?

I was at work when the call came to my husband. When he picked me up from work that night, he had a *Lonely Planet* travel guide of PNG lying on the front seat of the car. I asked, "What is this?"

He replied, "That is where we're going."

Without hesitation, I asked, "Oh? When can we go?"

I was so excited about working for the Lord that I didn't care *where* we went. I just wanted to go. Adventures waited! Little did I know the troubles and triumphs that awaited us in this land of Papua New Guinea.

It was six months later before we finally set foot on PNG soil. The day after we arrived in PNG we were awestruck as we walked into their Headquarters' bamboo church. At the very front of the church were two banners: one of them said, "Welcome to PNG, Bro. and Sis. Henry." The other hanging below it stated, "The Islands Are Still Waiting…"

We were so amazed at how the Lord had prepared the way for us. So here we are, *still* in Papua New Guinea these years later!

God is so good. May you enjoy the stories we have to tell of this land far away.

CHAPTER 1
THE WAY IT WAS

April 5, 1973 was a day that the church in Papua New Guinea would forever look upon as a great blessing: Richard and Margaret Carver arrived with a call in their hearts to reach this nation with the Gospel of Jesus Christ. Moving from Australia, they brought their six-week old baby, Rachel, and moved into a very remote bush area of the Highlands. For six months they stayed with an independent church family in the village of Mai, Chimbu Province, and then moved five miles to the village of Gogol. It was in Gogol that they were able to build a house of their own.

The following year, the Carvers were blessed with a baby boy and named him Richard Jon. Richard Jon was born prematurely by two months, but the hand of the Lord was upon him, and he is now a young man who has followed in his father's footsteps.

Around the years of 1978-1979, the Carver family packed all their belongings and moved to the main town center of Goroka, Eastern Highlands Province. The work in Papua New Guinea is still headquartered in Goroka to this day.

Several years after moving to Goroka, an uprising began within the church ranks. By the time 1987 rolled around, the Carvers had to leave Papua New Guinea for their own safety, and for the sake of their children. It was only in April of 2002, that they returned for a wonderful reunion!

During that tumultuous time, Rev. and Mrs. Roscoe Seay were in PNG helping out the Carvers. Rev. Seay was beaten mercilessly, and yet held his head high as he represented the church in court until the final verdict – a win. Yet after only one year in PNG, they too, had to leave.

Those early years were years of great trial and tribulation: the rebellious faction that had arisen seemed to be winning, but the Lord gave us victory. Meanwhile, a Papua New Guinean national, Peter Dege, became Superintendent over the work when the Seays left. For seven years he helped hold this work together and there was a great time of revival. Sadly, Peter Dege resigned as Superintendent in 1996 to enter a life of politics. He is no longer a licensed minister with us.

At the writing of this book, there are over 230 UPC churches in Papua New Guinea and nearly 300 licensed ministers. The work grew incredibly in just a few short years! God has truly been blessing the Papua New Guinean church with unprecedented revival. The stories you will read in the following pages are just a small taste of what we have been through and witnessed over the years. We pray that our words will not only inspire, but entertain and challenge you as well.

The mission house in Goroka that the Carvers built, where we lived.

CHAPTER 2
A LETTER TO MOM

Dear Mom,

"Here we are in Goroka, PNG. It is 7:00 AM, and I am sitting at the dining room table with a banana and a cup of coffee. I just finished boiling our pot of water for the day. I was so tired yesterday, that I went to bed at 7:40 PM and just woke up an hour ago. Eleven hours of solid sleep. I must've needed it.

"It all started Wednesday night. We got to the check-in counter at the San Francisco International Airport, and we had a new girl wait on us. We were there two hours early and it was a good thing! She was very slow and had to get her superiors involved. After about 1½ hours we were finally able to get to our gate, just in time to board the plane. They charged us $600.00 for extra cargo.

"Our flight took off in time, and was the smoothest flight I have ever been on! All of these horror stories you hear of overseas flights proved wrong in our case. We felt as if we weren't even moving. The flight was 15 hours long, not including a stop in Honolulu, HI. We arrived in Manila, Philippines at 6:30 AM and by the time we cleared customs, it was 7:30 AM. The Sullivan's met us outside the airport, and we headed out to breakfast.

"The people in Manila drive like maniacs! On a three-lane road, they make it a five-lane road! If there is just enough room for your car, you squeeze in and honk your horn! Vendors would walk right in the middle of the road and sell papers, cigarettes, candy, etc. (Talk about drive-through shopping!) Manila is a city of about 15-million people. There is only one main road in the city for all of those people. I have never seen such a madhouse! I did my share of praying, that's for sure!

"After breakfast we stopped at a shopping mart then went to the Sullivan's home. They live at the Bible school complex, and have a very nice house. When we were ready to freshen up, the water had been turned off. They said it gets turned off every day from about 10:00 AM to 6:00 PM. I took a sponge bath, lay down and slept for a couple hours. (Manila is very hot!) We all had lunch together and then Bro. Sullivan's son took us back to the airport: another hour of "prayed-up" madness through traffic.

"We boarded the plane with no complications this time. We had a two-hour flight to Hong Kong, and a three-hour layover there. Hong Kong looked very beautiful at night! Nestled in the hills, and lights to match or beat Las Vegas! We stayed inside the airport and waited. We met some missionaries, native Papua New Guineans and tour groups on their way to PNG.

"Leaving Hong Kong about midnight, we had a six-hour flight to Port Moresby, PNG. I was asleep before the plane even left the ground. This was our second all-night flight and I didn't sleep well the night before. I slept continually for about 3½ hours and woke up at 4:00 AM (PNG time) to freshen up. At 5:00 AM, they woke everyone up over the PA system, and turned all the lights on. It was time for breakfast. We ate a very nice meal, and drank a good cup of homegrown PNG coffee.

"We landed in Port Moresby on time and had a greeting party to beat all! After checking through customs and paying duty on a computer we brought, we went outside the airport and were greeted with cries of joy, flower leis, hugs, and bilum bags (the native all-purpose woven sack the women use). This went on for about one-half hour. When we had hugged and greeted everyone, they all stood back and gave us a very big applause and followed us to the next gate. There was a tour group from Hong Kong present, and as Brian and I were the only people at the port being greeted in such a fashion, they kept squeezing in and taking pictures of the goings on! My, did we feel like royalty! As we entered the next gate, the others were not allowed in so they crowded up against the glass and waved and smiled. We waited in the gate lobby for boarding with another minister's family.

"When we arrived in Goroka, the Sinakadis were there to greet us. I stayed with Thecla Sinakadi, and Digi helped load our stuff into P. Dege's[1] 4-wheel. We then came to this house that the Carvers built. This is where we will live. When we arrived at the house, the local women had piled our kitchen counters full of fresh vegetables and all kinds of fresh fruit. Some of the fruit I'd never seen before and had to ask someone how to eat it and what is was called. A couple of local women came by to welcome us, but most of the evening we were left alone to rest and set up house. I was very thankful for that.

"That brings us to this morning. We are ready for church and will be leaving shortly (It is now 9:40 AM). I don't know what awaits us this day, but I will write later. Brian was asked to speak in both services today."

* * * *

"I am at home now sitting on the front porch. I just saw an ambulance go by – a white jeep with a red cross painted on the sides, and one red light on top. People here drive on the opposite side of the road (if they have a car, that is).

"It is cool and overcast. I hear distant thunder now and then, and I hope the rain holds off: my dryer doesn't work, and I just hung a load out to dry.

"Many, many people are walking by, the women with skirts on and bilum bags on their head. The men with pants/shorts and a Highlands hat or a baseball cap. There is a woman walking with a bundle balanced on her head, and she walks as if it weren't even

---

[1] P. Dege is the former national Superintendent of the PNG church.

there! Hardly anyone is wearing shoes, and if they do, it is only flip-flops or every once in a while, a pair of tennis shoes."

* * * *

"Let me tell you about church this morning: P. Dege picked us up at 9:50 AM. When we arrived at the church, many people were there to greet us. When we got out of his jeep, his wife greeted me, and so did the Assistant Pastor's wife. Other than that, all we got were stares and smiles! To be honest, it felt kind of awkward. We sat on the platform, of course, but not until after we had taken our shoes off.

"First, there was singing, we were introduced, then the Assistant Pastor led a couple songs before Brian preached. After the preaching, he asked for people who needed the Holy Ghost, or if anyone needed to be closer to God to come to the altar. Every one of the people responded. When done praying, P. Dege spoke a while about the salvation plan and about four ladies and 10 children came to the altar the second time. One of them received the Holy Ghost (not sure if it was woman or child). After church was over we got our big welcome from the saints of the Goroka Headquarters church, with hugs, handshakes, tears, and smiles.

"The Deges took us to the Bird of Paradise Hotel for lunch. Talk about a beautiful place! The outfits of the servers were blue skirts and tropical blue and white shirts (including the men – they wore the skirts, too!). Some wore shoes; some did not. Our server wore no shoes. I guess there is no place in PNG where you will see a sign that reads, "No shirt, no shoes, no service.""

"After dinner, P. Dege drove us around, and we went to a coffee plantation. We got out of the car and picked a coffee bean from the tree. It looks like a red berry of some sort. You break it open, and there are two beans inside. They are white and very juicy and sweet. You suck the bean to extract the meat and juice and then spit the bean itself, out. I never thought that a coffee bean would look like a tiny crab apple."

* * * *

"We have a dog, named Roo. You can see the poor thing's ribs. I plan on fattening him up as long as we're here. Just a few minutes ago, a child was walking past, dragging a stick of sugar cane along the fence to make a noise. Roo went running up to the fence barking his head off. Scared the poor child half to death."

* * * *

"Went to church tonight. This time I didn't have to sit on the platform. I sat next to M. Dege on the bamboo floor. They had a chair for me, but I didn't use it. I would have been the only one in a chair, and M. Dege would've set on the floor next to me. I didn't like that idea at all...so that chair stayed vacant. It wasn't really bad at all, to sit on the floor.

"One time, however, I heard something drop right in front of me from the tin roof, but when I looked I saw nothing. A few minutes later I moved my legs to change positions, and at the same time, tossed a huge black beetle out from under me! I didn't even know it was there! I whacked it with my shoe. End of bug.

"Toward the end of service a huge brown butterfly flew in and landed in front of me, off to the left, on the floor. Its wingspan was a good four inches. One of M. Dege's daughters went up to it and with quick movements, scooped it up. After church she "shared" it with her friends. What I mean by that, is they rubbed the wings all over themselves, and the sparkling color came off on their skin (and their clothes).

"As we were leaving the church, the children would walk really close behind me, and I felt them touch my hair (I wore it down), and then they would run away giggling. Then they did it again and dared their friends to do it. P. Dege said they have never seen such long hair, and are very happy to touch it. He said that when we go out to the market, they will touch it, hold it, and many will follow me, and they will come to church to see the missionary with the long hair!" [We have since learned how very true that is!]

* * * *

"It is now Monday, and we will be leaving for the market in about an hour. This morning we were rudely awakened by what seemed like a whistling teakettle going at a full scream! Brian hit his alarm, and nothing happened. We finally woke up enough to realize it was a flock of birds in the area[2]. When they called to each other, they sounded just like a loud, screaming teakettle! We started laughing, and then I grabbed my little tape recorder and went on the

---

[2] We quickly learned that this "bird" was not a bird at all. It was a large bug, a member of the locust family. The screeching noises we were hearing, were their wings rubbing together.

balcony to record their screams. I've never heard anything like it! They moved on, waking up everyone (including the roosters!)"

* * * *

"It is now Tuesday, at 2:10 PM. Yesterday, one of the women in the church brought over a beautiful little kitten! All black with white paws and chest, and the deepest blue eyes you ever did see. I noticed, however, that the little thing had a bad case of fleas. I gave it a bath, and cleaned off seven of them. Gave her another bath this morning and cleaned off two more. I thought, "Surely, that's the end of them." After she dried...you guessed it...at least three more. I let her walk around a little bit in the house to let her explore her world after her second bath. There is a really thin carpet layer over half the house, and I don't know if the house already had fleas and they jumped on her as she walked, or if they just clung on during her bath. When at the store looking for flea shampoo, I found out that no store carried it.

"I am going to close this letter for now. I will continue to write, and hopefully the next letter will be typed on the computer (it's not set up yet)."

"Love you with all my heart,
Esther"

* * * *

A week after the letter above was written, we took a trip up into the Chimbu Province - a two-hour drive from Goroka. It was there that yet another cat was given to us: a calico that we called

"Dindina". (We decided to name the black and white one "Princess.")

* * * *

In all these years, the letters home have never stopped. It wasn't until 1997 that PNG got this "new-fangled" thing called the Internet. What a wonderful change it made in our ability to correspond! Now we're hooked: we've got the digital cameras, the web pages, the works. It has made a world of difference in our friends' and family's ability to relate to our life here, and we thank God for it every day

CHAPTER 3
FRONT PORCH MUSINGS

Newly in the country, our favorite pastime was to grab a cup of coffee or a glass of iced tea and sit on the front veranda. This second story roost faces one of the busiest streets in town, and oh, the things witnessed from there! Recorded here are just a few of them.

* * * *

It totally amazes us to see the heavy burdens some of these women carry on their heads and backs. Living in PNG has made us realize more and more how spoiled we Americans are. The saying, "If you don't work you don't eat," is a stark reality here. They live off the land. Daily, we see the heavily laden women trudge by on their way to market.

As we take our trips along the Highlands highway, we see gardens on steep peaks, and women working them. They garden entire sides of mountains and then walk miles to market to sell their goods. Our heart goes out to them. Truly, if they don't work they will not eat. It's just a fact of life.

Occasionally, we see truck beds filled with men and women in their *bilas* (pronounced 'bee-loss') – the traditional paint, feathers, clothing (or lack thereof). They sing and beat their drums as they ride down the street. There are several reasons for doing this, and all are in celebration. They *bilas* whenever they are showing support for their electoral candidates, if there is a wedding, or perhaps a national holiday such as the PNG Independence Day.

From our front porch we've also heard mournful singing coming down the street. It could be drunken men locked arm in arm singing at the top of their lungs. It could be a group of mourners. We live directly across the street from the town hospital, so hearing the sound of mourning for the dead is a common occurrence. We feel like mourning with them every time we hear it. The sound of peoples' hearts breaking without hope is not a pleasant one. We can always tell how popular the deceased was by the sheer number of mourners. Sometimes if it is just a baby, we only see the mother mourning her loss, with perhaps one other woman at her side to comfort her. On the other hand, if a public figure has passed away, truckloads full of mud-caked mourners[3] will file past the house with red ribbons decorating each vehicle.

* * * *

The roads in town have not been maintained for several years and have turned into pot-holed dust strips. As our home sits

---

[3] "Mud-caked mourners" refers to the tradition the Papua New Guineans have of rubbing mud all over their faces (and sometimes their entire bodies) when mourning the dead.

just a few yards back from the road, a cloud of dust rolls toward us whenever a car passes. It is no longer a healthy pastime to enjoy "front porch musings."

In recent days there have been several promises to fix the road conditions in town. If those promises are indeed kept, we will once again enjoy the education we get by watching life from our front porch! There are still many occasions, however, when we will grab the camera and snap a photo of an important event, be it a *bilas* party or a full moon. There is rarely a dull moment when living in PNG!

A photo taken from the front verandah. This group was advertising their support for a particular political candidate. (Photo taken in April 2001) Dressing up and dancing is the customary way to do that, in PNG!

A great example of the women and young girls, carrying heavy loads in bilums on their heads. As soon as a young girl learns to walk, she begins to practice carrying a bilum in such a fashion.

CHAPTER 4
BON APETITE!

Much may be said about Papua New Guinean cuisine, and there are several jokes that we've heard over the years in regard to such. One of our favorites is the one about cannibals eating a missionary (it was their very first taste of religion). There are others dealing with *People Pot Pie, Cannibal Cobbler, Finger Foods*, and the puns go on.

At this point in time we are working among those who are only one generation removed from cannibalistic practices, and even today you'll hear rumors of it still happening[4]. If taking a trip to the local cultural museum just a few blocks from our house, you'll see dried finger necklaces and skeletal remains in bamboo coffins on display. These are memories of a time not so very far removed from today's culture.

Cannibalism aside, the normal day-to-day fare of the Papua New Guineans is actually quite healthy. Eight-five percent of the

---

[4] Reports of cannibalism are far and few between, and are mainly connected with the ultimate "payback" between enemies after a fight. Most of the time, issues are resolved (or not) with tribal fighting and village courts. Cannibalism is rarely practiced in today's culture.

population lives off the land, growing food of all varieties. Their main staple is *kaukau*, or sweet potato.

Up here in the highlands, any type of vegetable grows abundantly. After seeing the black volcanic soil that seemed to be its own version of *Miracle-Gro®*, I decided to test the fertility of the soil myself. One day I had eaten half a tomato and didn't want the rest. I took what was left and squeezed it along the fence in the back yard, and took a stick to stir up the soil a bit. Three weeks later there were tomato seedlings growing all over that area. The fertility of this soil and the rapid, steady growth of any seed amazes me to this day.

* * * *

Unlike grocery stores in most developed countries, our highland stores do not have large produce sections. There's really no need for it. Instead, we go to the main market where we can purchase any type of produce at very cheap prices, and the quality of the merchandise is very good. It truly is a paradise here in PNG, in terms of cheap, good quality produce.

One of the questions we get asked from visitors to PNG is in regard to whether eating greens here is safe. We are always delighted to answer them positively. Most all of the garden produce is organically grown and human waste is never used as fertilizer. The soil itself, and the natural process of vegetation decay that comes with a rainforest climate, is fertilizer enough. Needless to say, we enjoy greens and salads of all types that never make us sick.

* * * *

Perhaps the most far-fetched menu I ever consumed was snake. In June of 1995 one of our Bible School students found a huge green tree snake on his way home from a prayer meeting one night. The snake had a green back and a yellow belly, and was a good four or five foot long and about six inches around. These green tree snakes are much sought-after for food. On the street, one could get a high price for it.

Early the next morning we were awakened by whoops and hollers. Some of the students were having the time of their lives by letting the snake slither on students who were asleep, waking them up screaming in frenzy! They were being so loud and having such a good time, it woke us up, too.

After the commotion died down and they had their fun, it was time to eat it! In order to kill the snake for food, they cut it open while it was still alive to be sure that all the blood drained from it. Once cooked, the scales on the top part of the snake's body turned a vivid blue. They brought a little bit for me to try. Believe it or not, the meat was very mild and tasty…and to coin a redundant phrase - it tasted like chicken!

* * * *

The most consumed beverage in PNG is water. Many cannot afford soft drinks, juice, or any other beverage purchased in a supermarket. Ice-cold springs are abundant especially here in the mountains, and the nationals know which ones are safe for drinking. There have been times that we have showered under a cold mountain spring's waterfall, and drank the water as we showered.

It's terribly cold, but very refreshing! They also use these cold springs as refrigeration, by placing perishable items in banana leaves or plastic bags in the water. They will tie it to the shore or weight it with a rock so it doesn't float away.

Perhaps the second most common beverage is coffee. Coffee is the number one cash crop in Papua New Guinea, and nearly every village in the highlands has their own coffee groves. The coffee is mainly harvested around the months of May-July, and the monies received from selling the beans will be their mainstay throughout the year. Coffee is very valuable to these people, and is even exchanged along with pigs for bride prices[5].

It took us some time to learn the hospitality practices of PNG families. For example, if a family was in our home and we offered the adults some coffee, we would do the same for the children! Once children are weaned (usually between the ages of three to five years of age), they were "eligible" to drink coffee right along with the adults. The nights can be so very cold in these mountains and coffee may be the only thing on hand to warm their insides. It becomes "just another drink" to everyone in the family, regardless of age.

* * * *

Often we've been asked if there is a McDonald's restaurant in the country. There isn't a one! The closest one is a flight to

---

[5] A *bride price* is a ceremony in which the groom's family gets together with the bride's, and exchanges money, pigs, etc. as payment for her. After this ceremony, the bride goes to the groom's village, and they are considered married according to PNG culture.

Cairns, Australia. Needless to say, I do a lot of cooking from scratch and enjoy it very much. Overall, we have learned to value a good home-cooked meal. We love to try different ethnic fare (with caution), and there are several PNG dishes that we really love.

If you are interested in trying some ethnic PNG food, I have included some recipes at the back of this book for you to try. Enjoy!

With all the fresh vegetables available year round, and the abundance of large chickens, we usually have wonderful Thanksgiving meals!

My house lady (Grace) and I on the kitchen floor of our home, making PNG "karamap" – their version of a cabbage roll, using leaves from trees instead of cabbage.

CHAPTER 5
VILLAGE LIFE

Village life, for the most part, is very peaceful and quiet. The sense of family and community/tribe is very strong. Their huts are quite close together and are shared by all, and they have somewhat of an "open house" policy. Anyone within the village can come and go from each other's homes as they please.

An average morning begins with a small breakfast of *kaukau*, and if they're lucky enough to have an earth oven, perhaps some scones[6]. If they have company, they go all out and make sure they have instant coffee, bread, powdered milk and tinned margarine.

After breakfast it's usually time for a very cold bath in the mountain rivers. If the village is close to a natural waterfall, they can even take a shower! While they bathe, they will also fill huge containers with water and carry them back to the village. If they're lucky enough to have a tin roof in the village, then they can catch

---

[6] Scones are similar to dinner rolls, only they are fried in oil instead of baked

rainwater. The villagers treat rainwater as a great convenience: they don't have to walk down the mountain to the springs or rivers to collect it.

During the day the men either run errands or just sit around and talk, while the women work in the gardens and the children play. Life is very simple in the village. They lack most conveniences that you and I are used to, but they are contented and happy for the most part, in their daily routine.

* * * *

Fire, of course, is an absolute necessity in village life, and the good thing about it is that it's free! With westernization, however, kerosene has become very important, and nearly a necessity. They have realized the benefit of kerosene lanterns, burners for cooking, etc. If something is simply a "camping" product in America, it is a coveted life item for Papua New Guineans!

One evening as we were relaxing in a village hut with the local pastor's family, the pastor's wife was trying to light their kerosene burner, but didn't have any matches. Her daughter simply went to the wall of their home, broke off a splinter of bamboo, and gave it to her mother. The pastor's wife took the splinter and stuck it in the flame of the little lantern...and viola! - A match to light the burner. These people are quite resourceful in making their lives reasonably comfortable.

Fire, water, and kerosene are the lifelines. They try to never let their fires die out, because they may not have matches available (the towns are located quite a distance from them). If ever their fires burn out, they have to send someone down the mountain to another village to "collect" the fire and bring it back up the mountain, or start their own the hard way – flint and dried grass.

* * * *

Watching Papua New Guineans prepare *mumus* (feasts cooked in the ground) is quite an education as to their ingenuity. Here's how they do it: A large hole is dug in the ground and slabs of wood are strewn across the mouth of the hole. River rocks are then placed on top of the wood and the wood is set alight. As the wood under the rocks burns and begins to crumble, the rocks fall into the pit and become red hot.

After the rocks are fallen, they remove the "dust" (ashes) and a few of the hot rocks. What is very fascinating is that, to remove the hot rocks, they take lengths of small branches and split them lengthwise -much like a split hair - and use them as *tongs*. They poke at the remaining rocks until all the ashes fall to the bottom. Banana leaves are then placed in the pit to cover the rocks. All the food (with the exception of the meat) goes on top of the leaves and is then covered with the hot rocks they had set aside. On top of this second layer of rocks, they will lay the meat. This second layer of rocks cook the meat and the juices run down to the *kaukau* and other vegetables or greens, flavoring them as they cook.

Then they cover everything in more banana leaves, sealing it off, so that even the smoke cannot escape. Now it just looks like a pile of leaves. They will leave it this way for at least two hours.

(However, they can actually leave it there until they're ready to eat it. The food will continue to slow cook in the extreme heat under the ground.)

* * * *

Using the toilet facilities anywhere in PNG is an adventure. If they have "modern" facilities in town, there is never any toilet paper, and the bathrooms are terribly unkempt and unsanitary. Every village has a small house, which is just their term for an outhouse. A very deep, narrow hole is dug in the ground and a small bamboo structure is built over it for privacy. Once that hole is all used up, they cover it and dig a new one. The Papua New Guineans are smart in the fact that they always dig their latrines away from any water source and downhill from their villages. They also keep the area inside the latrine covered in ashes from their fires, for sanitary purposes. (To be honest, we would rather use a village "small house" than some of the public facilities in town.)

When using a small house at night, however, just be careful! You must use a lantern or flashlight, because many times those who have gone before you didn't carry any light with them... and missed! Also during the rainy season a walk down to the small houses can become very treacherous. Many times, the ground becomes wet and slippery, and most times, the small houses are located "downhill" from the villages.

* * * *

The village churches are usually made of bamboo walls and dirt floors (with perhaps some dried grass as a covering). If they have a tin roof they consider themselves very fortunate indeed! Everyone sits on the floor without exception. Our churches are full most of the time, and they can squeeze more people into the building, if there are no benches or chairs. (The platforms usually have a couple of places to sit, whether it be wooden benches or chairs.) Plus, it is more convenient for mothers with small children to arrange them on the floor instead of trying to get them to sit still in chairs or on roughly hewn wooden logs!

Every time we travel and visit one of our village churches, it never ceases to remind me of the stories I've heard of the old brush harbor days, those early days of Pentecost. How the Fire of the Holy Ghost would fall on all gathered! How conviction was strong and no one resisted! That is very much the same thing that happens in our churches here in Papua New Guinea. They have barely enough to keep them alive and healthy, and that's all they ask. Every time we visit a village, we are awakened by the noises of men and women praying as the sun rises. When the roosters crow, it's time to pray. What a beautiful sound to hear first thing in the morning! They are very hungry for God's touch in their lives, and conviction is heeded! We could not have asked the Lord to send us to a humbler people. We are so thankful for that.

We have told many potential visitors to this country that if they have wanted to preach to a hungrier congregation, they wouldn't find it anywhere else. Preaching to Papua New Guineans is, by the most part, a very rewarding experience. They listen, believe, and then obey. They are ripe and ready for harvest!

Unearthing a "mumu"

A village house

CHAPTER 6
CULTURE SHOCK! – SHORT TERM

When most people think of the term "culture shock" they only think of the short term. There is a difference between short-term and long-term culture shock. Those who have lived overseas for any length of time will know what I mean. Granted, everyone experiences a little bit of culture shock when they first travel to a new place. Yet there is a shock that goes much deeper and is of a magnitude that will either make a person or break them.

Collected here are a few diary entries concerning our short-term "shocks". Although some of these stories are hilarious now, they were very much a shock to us then.

* * * *

Wednesday, December 7, 1994

Ever heard of a killer bee? Well, I think I've just seen one! At least it looked like it could kill! I was sitting on the front porch enjoying a glass of iced tea, when I heard a buzz and saw a bee that was close to two inches long, with little wings. It flew to the

43

bananas first, and I flew to the front door! I've never seen a bee so big.[7] Thank God for screens on windows!

Thursday, December 8, 1994

Today, as I peeled a couple bananas that were extremely soft (the best kind for banana bread), I discovered they were crawling with small maggots! Fortunately, although they were the same color as the insides of the bananas, they crawled around the brown, bruised parts – otherwise, I may have missed them! This is the first time that's ever happened to me. I've been having a lot of "firsts" lately.

I saw a little rat in my kitchen this evening! Dindina, our calico cat, was in the living room, so I grabbed her and took her to the corner floor cabinet where the mouse was. She sniffed and scoped out every inch! She could probably smell a fresh rat in the area, but couldn't find it. I found the hole it comes out, and placed a bit of cracker away from it, and left the cupboard door open. Once in a while, as Dindina and Princess were playing, Dindina would go into the kitchen to "check." The cats eventually wore themselves out playing, and curled up in the rocker to sleep. Wouldn't you know, a few minutes later that cracker totally disappeared? Smart little rodent, that one! I'm hoping Dindina will catch it! However, a

---

[7] These bees are not officially categorized as "killer bees", because they are not honey makers. They are a type of mud wasp, and if one stings you, you faint. If more than five attack you, the chances of you surviving are almost nil. There is no anti-venom that we know of. Thank the Lord for the survival instinct to run!

few nights ago, it ate half a banana while she was sleeping just a few feet away in the living room. Ever heard of playing "cat and mouse"? Well, it's going on in this house! If Dindina doesn't catch it soon, we'll have to set a trap.

Friday, December 9, 1994

Last night I opened a floor cupboard in my kitchen and I saw a white gecko lizard scurry away! First maggots, then rats, and now lizards (and there have always been plenty of roaches)!

Monday, December 12, 1994

Yesterday after the morning service, we were walking back to the truck, which was parked a block away because of the deep, muddy ruts leading up to the church. We had to walk past a neighbor's hut and garden, which was enclosed in wire fencing. An older woman standing by the hut saw me and jumped up and giggled and came running. I stopped and waited for her. I thought she would just shake my hand, but instead she bent down, reached through the fence and rubbed my leg! She then stood up and just grinned at me. I took her hand, and said, "Morning" and smiled. Boy, am I ever getting an orientation! Brian hasn't had any experiences like that – just warm handshakes, smiles, and normal hugs for him.

Saturday, December 17, 1994

Because Brian and P. Dege are out of town preaching, M. Dege came to spend the night with me. At 1:00 this morning, M. Dege woke me up, saying that Paul[8] was hollering to us from the front yard. She wasn't asleep because she was worried about a man who was in the hospital. Paul was informing us that he had just died.

After having phoned our husbands, we got up and went to the hospital across the street and went into the morgue where his body was kept. All the family had gathered around, along with a few elders from the church. The man's wife was anguishing, crying, mourning, and carrying on over the body, and so was her daughter. I've never in my life, witnessed such a display of emotion over the loss of a loved one. His sons simply turned to the wall and mourned in silence.

The morgue staff put the corpse on a gurney to get ready to take him to his house for a vigil, and by this time, it was 3:30 AM. M. Dege walked me home, and then went to the mourners' house with all the others. I went to bed. Paul came to check on me at 9:30 that morning. He hadn't gone to bed all night, and neither had anyone else. They were still keeping vigil with the family. At 5:00 that evening, P. Dege and Brian walked in the door of our house. They had left the Mt. Hagen conference early after they heard the news.

---

[8] Paul was our resident groundskeeper at the time.

After hearing the news of his death, Brian still had to speak at the conference in Mt. Hagen. He was not feeling up to it at all! His topic was the New Testament church, but the whole time, he felt as if he were talking to a brick wall. The people were not responding as usual. He felt like his words were going over like a lead balloon, when he began to speak of the Oneness of God, and the salvation plan for the New Testament church. When he finished teaching, he was feeling heavy, and knelt down to pray. As the alter call transpired, everyone came to the front and poured their hearts out to God! It really surprised Brian. Later when the question was asked if anyone wanted to be baptized in Jesus Name, around ten people raised their hands! After the alter call, one of those to be baptized came to Brian and said that he was a denominational pastor, was just visiting, and God had given him the revelation of the Oneness of God, while Brian was teaching! He said he now understood, and wanted to be baptized! Praise the Lord!

Also, two others received the gift of the Holy Ghost! It just goes to show, that no matter how you <u>feel</u>, God's word will never return void! Needless to say, Brian's heart was thrilled.

*　*　*　*

We set a rat trap tonight – there's no way Dindina can catch it in her condition: She got outside and our dog, Roo, chased her. When we brought her in we noticed her leg was broken. After chasing the vet down for 48 hours, we FINALLY got a cast put on her leg. Our little kitten, Princess is yet too small to be chasing after these big container rats – they almost dwarf her by comparison.

<u>Wednesday, December 21, 1994</u>

We waited until about 7:30 for a ride to church tonight (we are not about to walk after dark) and P. Dege never showed. So...we just went back in the house, confused, because Brian was supposed to preach! We finally heard a couple of people rattle the gate. Brian went down to inquire, and they said that church was canceled. When Brian asked, "Why?" they responded, "Because Bro. -------- died and everyone's still in mourning". No one had a phone and didn't bother to come to our home to let us know. I can already tell the lack of communication in this country is one of the things that we're not going to like.

<u>Monday, December 26, 1994</u>

Christmas in PNG is really "dull" when compared to the celebrations at home! No decorations on the streets, very few in the stores, and the only celebration in the church is to hold a weekend get-together. For our first Christmas away from home, the loneliness is really beginning to sink in.

We went to the Chimbu Province this past weekend to celebrate Christmas with our church folks there, by attending a gathering. While in Chimbu, one thing I noticed was that if some of the children had bites, they would scratch them raw and flies would swarm on their open sores. In the past, I've seen the same thing here in Goroka, but not to the extent of these remote areas. I've noticed that the flies land in their hair. I'm guessing because of the lice or some other parasite. A couple of kids had their heads shaven, with many sores covering their scalp. It is a common sight to see parents picking and grooming their children's hair to rid them of lice. Then many times the children would turn and do the same for the parents. This is quite a different culture, and takes some getting used to the social life.

<u>Wednesday, December 28, 1994</u>

My refrigerator went on the blink a few days ago, and when trying to contact a repairman, we had no luck. Everyone was "out of the office" until today, when the repairman finally came and fixed it.

What's kind of funny about the whole ordeal was that I had pressed some pineapple, put the juice in a jar, and put it in the refrigerator a few days ago. I wasn't aware of the refrigerator problem at the time. I got it out Sunday evening and there was foam on the top of it, and when I opened the lid, it sounded like pressure was released. I smelled it, and it didn't smell bad, so I poured some in a little glass and took a big sip. It had carbonation in it, and tasted to me, like pineapple soda! Paul tasted it, and said it tasted like a mix between pineapple wine and beer! Brian didn't have the nerve to try it. Needless to say, I dumped the rest.

* * * *

We had another tropical downpour this afternoon, which means we'll have to walk to church in the mud. If there is one thing I don't like about PNG, it is all the mud. It's everywhere, and it always wins!

Friday, December 30, 1994

When we went to the market this morning, I carried my bilum on my head like the rest of the women. It was really nicer than carrying the thing on my shoulder like a purse. That whole half of the market started hollering in Pidgin, "Hey look! White woman carrying a bilum on her head! Ayo!" (Laughter, smiles, etc.) I was very embarrassed and asked Paul if they thought it was absurd, or were they laughing for sheer pleasure. He explained it was the latter, because the PNG people are surprised when a foreigner comes into their country and does what they do. They were very happy. (Paul's explanations made me feel better, but I still took it off my head!)

On the way home from the market, I bought six dozen eggs at a little road-side stand and the people gathered around to watch this white woman pile all those eggs in a bag and fork over K15.00! I told the vendor that I used all these eggs to make banana bread, and I said it loud enough for the rest to hear, so they wouldn't think I was crazy!

Saturday, December 31, 1994

In three hours, fifteen minutes, the year 1994 will be over. Tonight is strange for us, because it is just like any other night. We have no watch night service. We were told that at one minute past midnight on New Year's Eve, there will be a great commotion, as people holler, sing, beat their drums, shoot their guns, etc.

* * * *

It is now six minutes after midnight. I hear the drums, the screams, the fireworks, etc. The only car that's been on the street is an ambulance and a police truck! Boy, is it ever <u>noisy</u>! Sirens, drums everywhere! Bells, whistles, horns. A police truck just parked in front of the house, and through a very loud PA system hollered "Happy New Year" and then fired a gun of some sort. It startled me so much, I let out a yelp, and Brian asked if I was OK (He was at the other end of the house). New Year is a <u>much</u> bigger thing to the Papua New Guineans than Christmas, and is also much more celebrated than what I'm used to back home.

It is now almost 20 minutes after twelve, and the noise is yet a crescendo. I'm going to try to get some sleep!
HAPPY NEW YEAR FROM PNG!

<u>Sunday, January 1, 1995</u>

We were on the way to church last week, and we heard some children in a yard shout, "Masta! Masta!" They were calling for Brian. Sometimes a white man is called "Master" and his wife is called "Mrs.". I personally don't care for the term. We are in no way superior to these people. We are all human and created in the image of God - we all have the same Creator! I guess that's just their way of getting the attention of a white man, but I still don't have to like it.

* * * *

Our rat trap has had the bait eaten off it three times, and only snapped once! Even then there was no rat! This one is definitely a smart one! I've seen a rat three times since being here; twice in the church, and just today, one lying dead in the road. Every time I've seen one, they've been as big as squirrels. I hope the rat in this house isn't that big; however, his droppings lead to the conclusion that he may be!

Saturday, January 7, 1995

Here I am, sitting on the edge of a very hard bed (nothing but a slab of wood on top of some stilts). At least we have a sheet of foam under us and a blanket over us. I was very thankful for that.

It is 7:20 AM and we are in a village in the Chimbu Province. I was up with the birds at 6:20 this morning. I was the first out of bed and was grateful; this made me the first one to use the bucket of rainwater we caught last night. There are seven of us sleeping in a little two-room cabin. Brian and I got the "bed" in one room, and the others slept on the floor on mats in the other room. We will all have to share the same water bucket this morning…now you can see why I was grateful to be the first one up!

We are quite high in the mountains, yet there are still some higher peaks. I looked out the window and saw such beauty when I awoke this morning! Layered between each mountain peak was a strip of cloud, and a patch of blue sky on the top of it all. The top strip of cloud had a pink hue to it because of the morning sun.

This cabin has no running water and no electricity. The rain was coming down so hard last night they canceled church. (They have church outside, because there is no shelter for the droves of people who attended this conference.) We all camped out in our cabin with a kerosene lantern on the floor, our substitute for a campfire. We ate hot kaukau and cooked lamb, and ate with our fingers, as usual. Some of the saints brought us fresh pineapple, strawberries, cucumber, cauliflower, bread, and Pepsi. We feasted, talked, and sang songs while another played a guitar. We had a grand time for four hours, when everyone finally retired for the night.

* * * *

On the way up to this village, we drove up a 4-wheel trail. Before we entered the trail, we asked a group of boys how the road was. They said, "Oh good! It's straight now!" What they meant by this was that the road had been flattened to take all the deep, muddy ruts out. We drove a little ways, and here was a rushing river in front of us, and the road went into it, and came out the other side! There was a police truck in front of us, and he made it across OK, so we just floored it and drove across the river. We stopped on the other side so I could take a picture of what we had just crossed. I was not going to lose that memory!

* * * *

Back home in Goroka…

Friday, January 20, 1995

Last night, Paul yelled at us from outside, to "come down quick, and bring a torch [a flashlight]!" We ran downstairs, and here Paul had hold of the tail of the biggest rat we'd ever seen! He had seen it crawl in between some pipes against the wall of our house, and grabbed its tail. With the light from our flashlight, he took a knife and wounded it, and drug it out between the pipes. It was huge! When Dindina got a hold of it she had the time of her life, but refused to eat it. One of the guys disposed of it, thankfully, and let the dogs have at it (they played with it, but didn't eat it either!). I had to take warm soap and water, and clean up the mess, after the guys and Dindina had their fun. Not a very pleasant job!

This morning a young boy came to me as I was typing this diary, and had in his hand a very small rat, and wanted to give it to Dindina! (Of all the things!) He kept insisting that it was a gift to our cat, so we let her have it. If she doesn't eat this one, I will NOT let them give her another one. Enough is enough!

* * * *

I think you get the idea of just some of the things that made an impression on us the first few months in the country. There is no way we have the space to write everything here, nor do we wish to bore you with too many details. However, what we want to convey at this point, is this: it didn't take long for us to get over the initial short-term culture shock. We gradually got used to the traditions, the bugs and other creepy-crawlies, and have even learned the positive benefits of some of the other traditions that were foreign to us at first.

Short-term culture shock was not necessarily a negative thing for us. Many times it was exciting, just because of the sheer newness of it all. It is the every-day, long-term cultural customs that can be trying. The next chapter deals with those aspects.

Brian baptizing in a mountain stream. Baptizing in rivers, streams, and the ocean, is the main method of immersion in PNG. People gather along the edge, or as you see here, sitting on boulders, and watch the baptisms. It's very serene and peaceful!

CHAPTER 7
CULTURE SHOCK! – LONG TERM

After the newness wore off and we began to get used to the culture, then the *real* shock set in. The daily frustrations of living in a third world country would get the best of us at times.

Before we ever came to PNG, we asked Loretta Scism[9] if she had any advice for us going into the mission field for the first time. Her reply was simple: "Be flexible and have a good sense of humor."

We have never forgotten her advice and always try to keep those very words in practice. Being flexible and having a good sense of humor is a necessity when facing challenges such as deep, long-term culture shock. It is an ongoing thing that you have to put up with for as long as you're on the field. (Our options are either to deal with it, or go insane. We prefer the former.)

To give some examples, let me share with you a few of the things that frustrate us the most:

---

[9] Loretta is the daughter of the former Global Missions Director of the UPCI.

* * * *

In Papua New Guinea, it is a victory if you can simply pick up the phone and speak to the person you wish to contact. Sometimes the phone lines are down, or that person is "out" or on another line. It is also very unusual if that person returns your call. In all the years we've been in PNG, we can probably count on our two hands the number of times that we have left a message and the call was returned. We're talking about people in the work force who are supposed to be professionals. Most of the time you have to call them back two or three times before you ever reach them, no matter how many messages you leave.

* * * *

Another frustration is the blatant discrimination against you, if you are an expatriate[10] in PNG. For example, if we are to ask the price of something on the street, they take one look at our skin color and double, triple, and even quadruple the price. It does help somewhat if you know their spoken language (Pidgin), because they'll find out you're not a newcomer and they can't take advantage of you. However, that doesn't stop their prices from skyrocketing far beyond the "native" price. There is no way to avoid that fact. It goes back to the common assumption, "If you're not rich, then how did you get *here*?"

---

[10] "Expatriate" refers to a person who lives outside their native country. Most expatriates in PNG are of European and Asian descent.

We have learned to work around the alternative pricing system by sending a national to do the "dibbling" for us, and sometimes it works. But if our liaison were to even mention that he's asking on behalf of their missionary... forget the good deal. It won't happen.

Also, as expatriates in PNG, we are high profile targets for thieves and beggars, and constantly have to be on alert. If it's not bolted down, it's going to get stolen. This past year it became necessary for us to erect high iron spiked fencing along the front of our property facing the street. We also had to install solid iron-sheet fencing along the side and back perimeters of our mission house. There is also a combination of barbed and rolled razor wire around the top of the fencing.

We have been the victims of robbery and vandalism more than we care to mention, but unfortunately, that's life in PNG. Papua New Guineans are very hospitable people to newcomers and visitors, and if just visiting, you can have the time of your life! But if you were to live here for any length of time, your chances of being robbed at some point are 100%. You may think this sounds harsh, but it is indeed a stark reality.

* * * *

There are several societies in the world today that are based on trust, and most of them are in developed countries where law and order reign. Papua New Guinea is not one of them. The motto here is that you do NOT trust, unless that person has proven himself or herself trustworthy. When we first came here - being of the trusting

American mindset - we were "taken" by con men more times than we care to imagine. We've since grown wiser. We are very careful with our money, the things we say and how we say it, because if we slip, there will always be someone ready and willing to take full advantage of us.

* * * *

Long-term culture shock can be a frustrating thing, because it seems that every thing about the country you live in can grate on your nerves. We began to experience this deep culture shock after our first deputation. We had been in America for a year, speaking of the work in PNG in churches all across the country. Of course, PNG was constantly on our minds. We had already lived on the field for several years, knowing the ins and outs of everything.

The honeymoon period was definitely over, and we knew it, but we had failed to prepare emotionally for our return to the field after deputation. Our attitude was one of "been-there-and-done-that" and we weren't prepared for the full brunt of immersion back into the culture. We had to do much soul-searching, praying, and gaining the victory. It took us nearly two years to get over that hump, after returning to PNG.

The same can be said about our return to our homeland after living overseas. Each time we return, we prepare ourselves to cope with the high-stress and demanding culture of America. Even *that* takes some getting used to. (In PNG our pace of life is much slower than it is Stateside, and if we're not careful, the stress of being in the USA can get the better of us.)

If there is any piece of advice that we can give anyone, it is to never expect that you already "know it all" regarding a particular culture. After being away from it for an extended period of time and then being forced back into it, you will always face a deep-seated culture shock unless you are aware of it and nip it in the bud to begin with.

On the positive side, one must always remember the benefits to living in a developing country, and more so, a tropical island! The pace of life here is so relaxing. People from developed countries come to places like PNG to get away from the hustle and bustle of life, and there's no better place to do it! Our Stateside families can attest to our complaints of the hectic schedule when we're at home. Not that we don't *love* the shopping and other conveniences, but we do end up missing the slower pace of PNG.

Also PNG's tight sense of family and hard work is a big plus. Everyone looks after each other. If one has a need, the others in the community come forward to help; whether giving of their garden vegetables, or building a home.

There are no orphanages in Papua New Guinea, because of the tight family situations. If a couple is unable to properly look after a child, or a child is born out of wedlock, other family members will take that child and rear him/her as their own. Abortion is unheard of. We've even been offered babies as "gifts". We have not accepted any of them, because of the "strings-attached" mentality to giving, in the PNG culture. That's another story all together, and we won't get into it here.

The fact that PNG is a beautiful tropical island can speak for itself. Papua New Guinea is directly located inside the "Ring of Fire" in the Pacific Ocean. The result is not only putting up with several earthquakes, but rich, volcanic soil! The flora and fauna of PNG, and the breath-taking landscape cannot be surpassed.

In summary, if you want a nice, tropical, relaxing vacation with plenty of revival to go around, Papua New Guinea is the place to be!

CHAPTER 8
BIBLE SCHOOL

We first came to PNG in 1994 expecting to build a Bible School facility, teach thousands, and change the country! Big ideals and large dreams are a good thing, when mixed with a little wisdom. However, we discovered that zeal without experience or wisdom can be very frustrating.

The first two years we shared our life with over 20 Bible School students living in the lower half of the mission facilities, 24 hours a day, seven days a week. There was no privacy whatsoever and our living quarters became familiar territory to the students. Don't get me wrong: we loved those students, and would have done anything for them, but it wasn't easy living in such conditions.

There has been delay after delay to our dream of building a respectable Bible School facility. When living in a country such as Papua New Guinea, patience is important-- you don't dare push too hard or you'll find yourself in a worse situation than before (we learned the hard way). But God is indeed good; and with patience, much prayer, and a little wisdom, the dream is becoming reality! Before telling you about our present Bible School project, however, let me tell a little of our first two years of teaching school in this country.

When organizing schooling of any sort, regulations are necessary, and you might be surprised at the kind of rules we had to enforce. Following are some of the "rules of conduct" for our English-speaking Bible School:

You Must:
1. Wear a tie to class.
2. Be clean-shaven.
3. Brush your teeth every day.
4. Have clean hands when you come to class.
5. Bathe or shower.
6. Talk English when you're on campus. No Pidgin!

Believe it or not, if we didn't check their grooming on a daily basis, they would ignore such simple procedures, and just show up "as-is."

* * * *

One afternoon I walked downstairs and saw one of our students sprawled out on the sidewalk. I thought he was dead! I shook him, and he awoke with a start.

He said that he didn't feel good at all, and was lying in the sun to keep warm. I had him come upstairs and laid him down on the spare bed, and he went right to sleep.

Four hours later Brian went to check on him, and he was still sleeping. He was lying on top of a thick quilt, and everything under him, clear through to the sheets and pillow, was sopping wet! Brian took his temperature, and it was 104.8°F! We put cold compresses on his head and chest, as Brian went down to get P. Dege.

By the time they came back upstairs and took him to the doctor, his temperature was down to 103°F. The diagnosis was malaria, a disease that is nothing to laugh at. Cranial malaria attacks the brain if it isn't stopped by medication.

Late at night a few days later, Brian and I were getting ready to call it a day. I was finishing up my project of shelling fresh peanuts to roast, and Brian was highlighting verses in his new Bible at the table. We heard a crash in the classroom below us, a startled cry, then a roar of prayer. A minute later Paul yells at us; "Come quick! George fell down and he's dead!"

"O.K. I'll get my clothes on," said Brian. (He was wearing his robe).

"For goodness sake, Brian, just go in your robe! Who cares! And hurry!" I exclaimed.

He ran downstairs and I ran into the bedroom to fetch my robe, adrenaline pumping at full speed! "George, dead?"

I ran down to the classroom in time to hear Brian yell, "One of you go across the street to the hospital and get an ambulance, and someone else run to P. Dege's house and fetch him!"

The students just stood there in shock.

"GO! NOW!" Brian stirred them to life, and off they went.

At this point I had reached them, and I was taken aback by what I saw. George was lying on his back on the floor between the desks, with a wooden stick and a red marker protruding out of his

65

mouth! It looked like he had fallen, and the stick had protruded his throat! After one of the students removed the wood and marker, it dawned on me that he had simply had an epileptic seizure as a result of battling malaria for many years. John, the class vice president, recognized the seizure and picked up the wood and marker to stick it in his mouth to keep him from swallowing his tongue.[11]

The red marker sure made things look like the wood had protruded his throat, because George was biting down so hard on the marker, it opened, and what looked like blood was coming out of his mouth! After the ambulance came and took him to the hospital, we sat and talked until our adrenaline slowed down a little, then we began to laugh: a red marker indeed!

We explained to our students what causes an epileptic seizure. Some of the students blamed witchcraft and sorcery – which is very common in PNG – for George's health problems. Apparently he was given some kind of "potion" when he was a child. The Papua New Guineans call it "spoiling the child." Sorcery and witchcraft are a very powerful force here in PNG, and we have heard many stories from people in the church of things that happened to them in the past. The stories would make your blood curdle! But the Lord has saved them and put a hedge of protection around them. Because of their belief in the power of the blood of Jesus and their lack of fear, nothing can hurt them. That's our God!

---

[11] It is important to note that sticking something in a person's mouth to keep them from swallowing their tongue during a seizure is very dangerous, and should not be done!

When He saves you, He gives you total peace and love, therefore dispelling fear!

At any rate, George had to go home that week because of his medical condition. To this day, he has trouble with reasoning skills and seems to "lose himself" in social circles. It was very hard to see one of our most eager students reach that point, all because of malaria. At least his life was spared, and we thank God for that.

* * * *

July 18, 1996 was an evening we'll never forget. The Bible School's Class President, Kopsy Komane, came and told us that Thomas Kunda, another student, was in the hospital from stab wounds! His wife had stabbed him twice, with a seven to eight inch knife blade. She got him once in the upper left arm, and once through the back, on the side of his heart.

Brian went immediately to Ward 2 of the hospital. He saw Thomas covered with blood and sitting in a chair, an IV stuck in his arm. He was going into shock. Brian said that Thomas was having a very difficult time breathing, and was shaking.

Thomas whispered that the doctor who examined him said, *"Sapos emi dai, emi samting bilong em yet!"* (Translated, it means literally, "If he dies, that's his problem!")

Brian was very angry with the callousness for human life, and demanded to know the name of the doctor. The nurses claimed ignorance, saying, "It must've been a doctor that worked a different shift." (Welcome to the wonderful world of the Goroka hospital!)

After a time of prayer, Brian sought out P. Dege, and they left for the Chimbu Province to send word to Thomas' family.

I stayed up and waited for them to come back. Brian walked in the door at 1:30 AM. They had stopped off at the hospital on the way home, to see Thomas. He had a bed, they had stitched up his side and bandaged his arm, but both were still covered with blood! They didn't even try to clean him up.

Brian related this story to me: as they journeyed up the highway to see Thomas' family, there was a police checkpoint on the border of our province and the Chimbu province. The Chimbu province at this time was a "dry" province, and they confiscated all liquor from passing vehicles. (The police, many times, drink up whatever they confiscate!) At this particular checkpoint, they made the guys get out of the vehicle, and dug around in our car, thoroughly checking everything. Finding no booze, they allowed them to proceed.

In between the first checkpoint and the border, thugs jumped out in front of the car! There were three, and two of them were drunk. They kept trying to get the car keys, but fortunately, Brian took the keys out of the ignition and held them tight. One drunk went to Brian's side of the car and demanded money in a loud, slurred speech. Brian simply sat there and looked straight ahead. (He had to fly to an island province the next day, and his wallet was loaded with traveling money!) This whole time, P. Dege was trying to talk them out of doing what they were doing, in their own tribal language.

Brian got fed up with the whole ordeal, and in Pidgin, he said, "Look! I have come 17,000 kilometers to this country to do a work for the Lord. Right now, we have an emergency and are on our way to Chimbu to carry news to a family. Please let us pass."

The thugs thought about this and the one that was sober, stuck up for them. This made the other two mad, and they began to fight among themselves! Brian simply stepped on the gas and drove off while the rascals fought. The thugs didn't get a cent from them! We thank the Lord for His divine protection!

Up the road a ways was another police checkpoint, but one of the policemen was a brother in our church and just let them pass without incident.

Once reaching Thomas' area, they told his pastor the news. Because of the late hour, he in turn informed the family. He also said this was the third time they've had problems with Thomas' wife. His words were, "She is a very wicked woman."

Because the men got home so late that night, I took Brian's class the next morning. When we gathered for class, I asked about Thomas. The students said he was doing better, and was also able to breath a little better. Thomas had also requested a divorce from his wife.

At present Thomas is still unmarried, but alive and well, thanks to the healing power of God! What his former wife is doing today, we have no idea.

* * * *

One day the Bible school students had nothing to eat, and it was only after I questioned one of them that we learned this had been their third consecutive day without food! They liked to fend for themselves, so we let them, but we weren't prepared for them to keep their hunger to themselves! We gave our groundskeeper some money to buy us a bag of flour so I could make some bread. With the change, we told him to buy sweet potatoes for the students.

How our hearts ached to see these students go hungry, and there wasn't much we could do about it at the time, being on a very sparse AIM budget. We couldn't feed even one, because it wouldn't be fair to the others. All we could do was pray.

Prayer worked, however, and ladies' groups from the local churches began to feel compelled to help with food! From that day on, the students never went hungry!

* * * *

The following story does not relate directly to the Bible School students, but goes along with some of the difficulties we had those first couple of years:

We had two dogs, one that was here when we came (Roo) – and the other was given to us as a tithe. The scrawny, sickly, neighborhood dogs began to find their way into our yard as soon as they found out we were an easy food source. We just couldn't keep up the bill to feed them all. We stopped buying dog food all together. Whenever I cooked a chicken, I took what meat I wanted and split the rest, bones and all, between the two dogs. Any leftovers we didn't eat went to them, too.

We thought the Bible School students were giving them rice once in a while, but after finding out that they were not even getting enough to eat, that possibility was shattered. The dogs were only getting bones or whatever we could give them. They hungrily gobbled the few scraps that we threw on the ground.

I didn't realize how hungry the dogs really were, until one day when I dumped the cats' litter box into the fire pit outside; Roo began to eat their droppings! The smaller dog tried to get his nose in it, but Roo growled, and the smaller dog had to give up.

I ran upstairs, and after my stomach calmed down I grabbed all the canned cat food I had and gave it to the smaller dog. To Roo, I gave half a cooked chicken that I was saving for soup. They gobbled up their portions, which disappeared in only about a minute.

Thankfully the Lord was merciful to all of us and began to *abundantly* provide our needs. Now, when I cook for just the two of us there is always more than enough for another hungry soul or two.

* * * *

The crowded conditions of the combined school and mission house, the lack of cooking facilities and the lack of privacy, forced us to make the decision that we could not have Bible school sessions in Goroka until new facilities are built. There was no choice. However, we did remodel the classroom downstairs to be used as a meeting room, and for short-term day classes. But a full-fledged, on-campus Bible School cannot happen at this time.

At present, the Lord has blessed us with a prime, five-acre piece of property on the outskirts of town. Because of the generosity of Christian Life Center of Stockton, CA, we have been able to buy this property and have the funds to get the ground preparation work completed.

The classroom which was used for Bible School, underneath the mission house.

CHAPTER 9
SETBACKS

By Brian Henry

If you have been in the church for any length of time, you have no doubt experienced your share of setbacks. Trials, tribulations, and difficulties are an intrinsic part of the Christian experience. Sure, we love to talk about the good times, the victories and the miracles, but the sweetness of those good times is often enhanced by the remembrance of victories won under extremely difficult circumstances.

The Papua New Guinean believers have had their share of setbacks since the beginning. However, during those trying times, they have witnessed the hand of God bringing deliverance in a very real way.

In 1987, a group of men, motivated by a hunger for power, rose up within the church and caused great division. Eventually things ended up in national court, as they attempted to seize control of the church. The Richard Carver family had to leave the country for their safety. Missionaries Rosco and Mary Seay came to PNG to assist in the work, but were also forced to leave after several death threats and Brother Seay being severely beaten. After the Seays left, the work went seven years without a resident missionary. Eventually, the church won its legal battles and the breakaway church slowly deteriorated to nothing.

I should point out that other church groups have also experienced these difficulties. It seemed that a spirit of radical ultra-nationalism, which affected more denominations than just ours, was sweeping the country. Through all of this, the hand of the Lord was still upon the Church.

When Esther and I arrived in PNG, we heard about the difficulties in the work. We also knew about the former missionaries' inability to stay. We felt that the work had two strikes against it and it would be unlikely another missionary would be sent to PNG, if we also were forced to leave. It seemed that the onus was upon us to break the back of that rebellious spirit, and the task was daunting.

Our first few years in PNG were much like a honeymoon. We enjoyed a wonderful move of God, and the churches were growing. We began to think that perhaps we would escape the difficulties experienced by the previous missionaries.

In 1997, however, the honeymoon ended. The resignation of our National Superintendent to pursue a political career marked the beginning of three very trying years for the church and for us, personally. To really appreciate the difficulties involved, it is important to understand politics in Papua New Guinea. When a man runs for a political office, his entire clan is culturally obligated to support him. This means that some pastors even abandon their congregations for two to three months to support their *wantoks* (pronounced, "one talks").[12] The wantok culture is the basis of the deep-rooted corruption in politics, government operations, election-related violence, and has also affected the church. We have to constantly fight the wantok system in order to develop the church here. If a wantok wins an election, the pastor supporting him is likely to leave the ministry altogether. For this reason, the church in PNG has had a long-standing policy to discourage pastors and ministers from contesting in political elections.[13]

During the 1997 elections, we were very concerned about a negative precedent being set for the church. Several of our pastors, following the lead of the former Superintendent, left their churches to run for parliament and local level governments. Many of those churches were forced to close down due to tribal fighting or the lack of a pastor.

Shortly after the elections, Esther and I went back to the States for our first furlough. It was difficult to leave PNG, because our hearts were greatly burdened for the work. However, budget needs dictated that we come home. The Lord prospered our

---

[12] A *wantok* is a very close friend, or someone who speaks your language. People in leadership generally give preference (whether deserved or not) to their wantoks. There are over 700 different languages in PNG, so you can just imagine the division and confusion that a wantok system brings into everyday life.
[13] In 2002, PNG held another election. Over 3,000 candidates consisting of over 40 political parties were competing for 109 seats in the national parliament!

deputation and we were able to get back to the country in less than a year.

As 1998 drew to a close, we entered the new year prepared for conflict. What we left behind as a simple difficulty evolved into full-scale spiritual warfare in 1999. Another breakaway had formed during our absence, this one being led by a man who was very close to us; one who ate at our table, one whom we called a friend. During that year after we returned from furlough, we were threatened and harassed. We traveled around with a constant knowledge that danger and harm could come upon us. It was like walking around with a large bulls-eye painted on us.

Things really came to a head during the September minister's conference of that year. Little did we know what that weekend had in store. During the Saturday morning service, we noticed a lot of activity going on outside of our Headquarters church. We all knew that something was going on in the spiritual realm. The enemy was up to something and had planned all year to strike at this time.

We were blessed to have Robert Forbush and missionaries David and Kathy Brott with us during this time, and they were a great support. Bro. Brott was preaching the morning service and was mightily anointed. He had basically scrapped his notes and was dealing with the spirit which had reared its ugly head. As the service drew to a close, we leaders formed a single line with Bro. Forbush leading the way.

As we left the building, the factious group was gathered outside with the former superintendent (their ringleader) as their spokesman. They had even changed the lock on the gate to the church grounds and were effectively holding all 300 of us hostage! We knew they were trying to pick a fight. They wanted an excuse to beat us up and have us deported from the country. As words were being exchanged, it was amazing to witness the spirit of calm that descended upon our ministry. This breakaway group was just a small, vocal bunch of power-hungry men. The ministry knew this and the Word of God that was preached in the morning service was like a soothing ointment.

After threatening them with court action for illegally holding us hostage, they unlocked the gate to let us go. Going back to the house after this service, we were extremely discouraged. Esther sat at the kitchen table and began to read her Bible as I sat on the living room sofa and began to complain about our present predicament.

I said, "Esther, we have a wonderful pastor and church family in America that love and appreciate us. Why don't we just go home? No one's forcing us to stay here."

As soon as I uttered these words Esther's eyes fell upon the next passage of her Bible reading: Ecclesiastes 10:4: *"If the spirit of the ruler rises against you, do not leave your post...."* (NKJV) As she shared this scripture with me, we both began to thank the Lord for speaking to us and for giving us the courage to endure.

A mere three weeks after this incident, the former superintendent flew to the capital city to try to get us kicked out of the country. However, the immigration officer would hear none of it, and even threatened legal action against him if he harmed us in any way! (God had allowed a faithful minister to witness the accuser entering the immigration office, and he was able to immediately refute the false allegations brought against us.) We were grateful to an all-seeing God who spared and protected us during that time.

Today, for the most part, that spirit has been broken. Esther and I often reflect on those hardships with a deep-seated joy and satisfaction in knowing that God will defend His own. It is wonderful to see the hand of God in such a deep and personal way.

Think of the hardships the Apostles faced. They had great revival, but they also endured great hardship. We often say that we want revival, but are we willing to be mocked, misunderstood, and betrayed? The road to revival is riddled with potholes and blind curves. Those who experience it must be willing to endure a difficult and trying journey. You will not find revival on Easy Street! The Scriptures are full of examples of God's blessings in the face of seemingly impossible obstacles. This is another perspective of missionary life; the reality is that great persecution produces great revival. It's the knowledge that if we suffer with Christ, we shall also reign with Him. For those who desire a greater move of God in your church or personal life, I would encourage you to get out of your comfort zone and trust in the Lord to bring you to a deeper dimension. How wonderful it is to know that our God is always faithful!

CHAPTER 10
MIRACLES NEVER CEASE

A preacher we heard in the States once spoke on miracles, and something he said really stuck with me. He said that many people *want* a miracle, love to hear *about* miracles, think they *deserve* one... but very few are willing to *need* a miracle. Wanting a miracle and needing one, are two different things. Most miracles only happen when our backs are up against a wall and we are in dire need of divine intervention. How many of us are actually willing to get to that place? Although we indeed have been in situations like that, we do not like the idea of being there! However, it is during those times that the Lord comes through.

There are countless times in PNG when we felt we needed divine intervention, though sometimes God answered with silence. Yet, it always works out for the best when God's in charge! Let me relate just a few miracles that have taken place in our lives these past few years.

* * * *

At least every other day we must boil a big pot of water. One day I had done just that, and was using a ladle to pour the water into a couple of cups to make some instant coffee. I missed the cup, and boiling water cascaded over my hand, and trickled down underneath my wrist. Immediately my hand and arm began to turn red. I looked at my hand and hollered, "In Jesus Name, don't you burn!" I never had an ounce of pain, the redness went away in just a couple minutes, and my hand returned to normal.

God knew that when living in an area where emergency medical service is practically non-existent, He must take over, and indeed He did for me that day!

* * * *

June 13, 1995: worry settled over me as I waited for my husband to return from a coastal city, where he had traveled for the weekend. He was traveling with P. Dege and Rev. Rex Deckard[14]. The guys had gone down there to purchase a few carvings from a village that is known for their exceptional artwork. Rex Deckard's wife, Brenda, and I were quite anxious about our husbands being gone so long, and to our chagrin, they did not arrive home until 4:00 AM the next morning.

When they finally arrived home, Brian told me what happened. On the way up into the Highlands from the coastal valley, they hit a thick patch of fog in the area where rascals[15] hang out. It was very late at night. They decided to shut the car off and sit and wait for another car to come so they could continue on together for protection. They sat there for 15 minutes, and no cars

---

[14] The Deckards were short-term mission workers here in Papua New Guinea in early 1995.

[15] Whenever you hear the term "rascal" in PNG, it refers to criminals and/or mischievous thugs.

came. At that point they decided to continue on. A little further on they saw that the fog had cleared at the top of the pass. There in the road was a semi truck that had flipped, with its loaded cargo partially hanging off the steep ravine at the edge of the road. It was a fresh accident, and the people were still inside the truck, in shock, trying to get out. The truck had jack-knifed and slid on its side for quite a ways. It was then that the men realized that if they had not stopped and waited those fifteen minutes, they could have, and most probably *would* have been caught in the middle of that semi truck's mishap.

They stopped and helped the people out of the truck, smelling alcohol everywhere. The victims with the driver were two "highway meris" (prostitutes). The driver said his brakes went out, but Brian said they were also saturated with alcohol. He helped one of the ladies out of the truck who just clung to him like her life depended on it! She was in shock, and Brian began to pray for her.

By the time everyone was rescued, the men continued on their way. Brian said his hands smelled like beer, that woman was so drunk. Of course, they could have had beer in the truck and during the accident, some of the bottles broke and spilled on them, but they were also drunk.

We thanked God for a safe journey for our husbands.

* * * *

In September of 1995, I stayed awake until late one evening, waiting yet again for my husband to return from the remote province of Chimbu. A trip that should have taken only four hours took seven, because of car trouble. They ended up having to creep back to Goroka with only third gear, and 4-wheel drive. They didn't even have reverse. It was nothing short of a miracle that they made it to Goroka. At one point, as they were crossing a bridge, rascals blocked the road! Instead of stopping, they tried to keep going at their snail's pace, and those bandits either had to jump out of the way or get run over.

The rascals got angry and began stoning the car as they passed. P. Dege was the driver of the vehicle and had enough! He stopped the car. Both he and Brian got out and began to walk toward the rascals standing in the road. Rascals as they may be, they were also cowards! They began to scatter and hide in the bushes along the edge of the road.

P. Dege and Brian just stood there and waited until the rascals realized they were not holding weapons and they began to come out of hiding. Once they were assembled, P. Dege let them have it, and didn't leave until everyone of them apologized!

I laughed as Brian related the story, then he added the best part: P. Dege told the men they were "on a mission for the Lord, and reminded them that this highway doesn't belong to them, it belongs to the government for *all* the people... and how dare they stop him and act this way...", etc.

One of the rascals, when P. Dege mentioned they were on a mission, had the nerve to say pleasantly, "Oh, I go to church, too", as if it would score points in his favor. By this time the thugs had calmed down and listened to reason, and let our preachers go.

It was indeed miraculous that they survived being held up by rascals and the lack of gears, especially in these mountains!

* * * *

The following account has been published in other periodicals and books, but this being my own manuscript, I wanted to relate the story again. I like to refer to this story as "Japheth's Miracle":

On Sunday, March 10, 1996, after our morning worship service, a young couple asked us to pray for their baby. This couple lived in a remote village and attended a denominational church. Their baby had been very ill for five weeks, so they came to us for prayer.

The baby's name was Japheth. He was only six months old, but he was at death's door. He had had severe diarrhea, vomiting, and urination problems for five weeks. His eyes were sunken, his belly was extremely swollen, and his ribs stuck out like a skeleton. In addition, he was severely dehydrated. As I cradled that precious baby in my arms and prayed, I could feel that his skin was burning up with fever.

Japheth was in my thoughts continually. The next day I woke up with him still on my mind. As I prayed, I asked God what I should do to help that little child. I searched through the book entitled, *Где There Is No Doctor*[16], and became inspired as I read

---

[16] David Werner, *Where There is no Doctor – A village healthcare handbook;* Revised Edition 1992 (The Hesperian Foundation, P.O. Box 1692, Palo Alto, CA 94302 USA).

about preparing rehydration liquids and about the care of infants with high fevers. Everything I was reading seemed to be just the prescription that Japheth needed!

Brother Walu, the man who had brought the couple to church, also drove a town bus. After going to the market, buying some bananas, and preparing a liter of rehydration liquid, I sat on my verandah and waited for his bus to come to the bus stop across the street. When his bus came, I ran across the road and asked Brother Walu where the family was located. He informed me that they were staying with the baby in Ward 4 of the hospital. I immediately went to Ward 4, only to find that the family had taken the sick baby out for a walk.

At 2:00 PM I returned to Ward 4, and Japheth was sleeping soundly with an IV in his arm, his mother using the respite to take a shower. I sat on the edge of his bed, as a roach and a spider crawled on the wall near his head. I touched his little feet. There were cool to my touch, but the upper portion of his body was still very hot.

When his mother returned to his bedside, I explained the rehydration drink to her. I asked how long Japheth had been in the hospital. She said, "Off and on for six weeks."

I asked, "How long have they been giving him glucose water via IV?"

She replied, "Just now, this afternoon…for the first time."

I was outraged at this information, knowing this hospital sometimes had the reputation for a total lack of concern for their patients. One good thing I learned from Japheth's mom, however, was that when they came back to the hospital after church Sunday morning, little Japheth smiled and cooed for the first time in over a month. She believed that God had already healed the source of the sickness and that the healing of the diarrhea and vomiting was only a matter of time! I was amazed and encouraged by her faith.

The following day, two days after we prayed for him, he had already downed a half-liter of the liquid and didn't vomit once. I touched his skin and his fever was totally gone. The diarrhea had also stopped.

Japheth left the hospital in just under a week, completely healed of his sickness and gaining weight. I was so very thankful to the Lord for healing him, and for giving us the wisdom to do the right thing by giving him that special liquid. I told his mother that we needed to be thankful that we served a great big God!

"Oh, yes!" she said. "Every morning when I wake up, throughout the day, and when I go to bed at night, I thank the Lord for healing my baby!"

* * * *

National Conference April 2001: The people gathered in the mud and rain with such hunger in their hearts! Thousands of them! As the worship and singing went on, and the preaching went forth, not a single person left. They were all focused on what was happening, and listening intently to every word. There was such great faith in that place! It radiated throughout the crowd. Rev. Doug Klinedinst spoke incredibly faith-building words to us all, and it was definitely efficacious!

There was a call for healing, and everyone was in one mind and one accord. A man walked to the front on crutches, a blind man came, a mother carried a lame son to the front, and they just kept coming. People with needs of all sorts came to be healed of the Lord! Not all of them needed a "visible" touch, but they all needed a miracle.

The worship began to crescendo to Heaven, and what a deep, powerful move of God we had! It was pouring rain and everyone was soaked from head to foot. They were standing or kneeling in ankle-deep mud, oblivious to it all! All they thought of was Jesus and His power to heal. The miracles began to take place, one here and one there. The young man who came on crutches was able to stand on his own two feet, however wobbly at first. But as the worship continued, he gradually gained a steadier step.

The blind man who came to the front was healed! He could not, and would not shut his eyes! Oh, how I wish I could describe the look on his face, as for the first time in perhaps many, many years, he could see clearly! Someone went to "high-five" him, and it startled him so much, he instantly reacted and grabbed the man's hand as it flew through the air. He was so surprised at his own reaction that he began to dance and rejoice! Before that night, he would not have even been able to see nor react to someone wanting to greet him in such a fashion.

The mother with the lame child who could not walk, calmly disappeared into the crowd.... with her child walking behind her! She was so overwhelmed at what the Lord had done; she was in shock, I think. One of the crusade team members went down to her and asked her if the Lord had healed her boy and she said that He had!

Two other men had very serious illnesses that they had battled for weeks, including high fevers, weakness and all sorts of difficulties. We knew them and so we knew they were speaking the truth. That particular night, however, the Lord healed them, gave them strength, and one man even began eating again after almost three weeks of being unable to keep anything down but liquids.

That conference was so mightily blessed of the Lord. We had been fasting and praying for God to do just what He did! We have had to fight so many spiritual battles here, and Brian has often prayed, "If we are going to have to face Apostolic persecution, then Lord, please let us see Apostolic results!" The Lord indeed answered that prayer.

* * * *

Let me tell you the miracle of "the robe." I bought the material and made a bathrobe with my own hands, when we still lived in the States. I know every stitch and detail of that robe. At the particular time this story begins, the bottom of the right belt loop had become completely detached from the garment and was hanging loosely from the threads connected to the top of the loop. The belt loop on the right side would not hold my belt and therefore, when I removed my robe, I'd have to tuck my belt into the left pocket until I wore it again. That right belt loop was useless, and had been for months. I did not have a stitch of thread in the house to match the color of my robe, and my sewing machine was completely covered up and put away in a closet in the spare bedroom.

Those few weeks before going back to the States for our first deputation, we had been facing some especially difficult times. One night, very late, I lay on the bed, crying out to God, giving Him every single thing that was worrying me. Still feeling a little despondent, but assured and thankful of His answering my prayers, I went to sleep.

I awoke a 5:30 the next morning and lay there on the bed listening to the early morning creatures and hearing a steady rain. It was very peaceful, and I decided to get up and celebrate the morning.

After thanking the Lord for a beautiful day, I opened my closet and reached for my robe, which was hanging on the same hanger, in the same spot where I had hung it the previous day.

Without turning on the light, I reached in and grabbed it.

I donned the robe and, out of habit, went to reach into my left pocket to grab the ends of my belt. They weren't there! In the darkness I felt around the waist of my robe, and lo and behold, my belt was hanging in *both* of the loops as they were supposed to be. The right loop was, as I felt with my right hand, completely and professionally sewn on, and the belt was resting through it and hanging normally.

My heart began to pound in my chest, and as gently as I dared, I woke Brian up and asked, "Hey! Did you fix my robe?"

He groggily replied, "What? I didn't even know it was broken."

I sat on the edge of the bed and told him as calmly as I could, but I was shaking. By this time, he too, was wide-awake.

I went to the bathroom and turned on the light to examine this mystery loop. It looked as if it had been sewn on by machine with the exact color of thread to match the robe. It was done so perfectly, I know it had to be the work of a Professional! We knew for a fact that neither of us could've done this ourselves. It was a miracle from the very hand of God Himself!

Why would God be concerned about a broken belt loop on a little missionary's bathrobe, and what does that have to do with answered prayer? I believe the Lord woke me up early to see His miracle, to let me know that He heard all my petitions I brought before Him the night before. I still have that bathrobe, and the long "starter" thread still hangs from one end of that patched belt loop. (I couldn't bear to cut it off!)

* * * *

To wrap up this chapter, I want to leave a poem with you that never fails to inspire me when times were tough. When you're in desperate *need* of a miracle, please don't give up just before it happens!

DON'T QUIT

Don't quit when the tide is lowest,
For it's just about to turn;
Don't quit over doubts and questions,
For there's something you may learn.

Don't quit when the night is darkest,
For it's just a while 'til dawn;
Don't quit when you've run the farthest,
For the race is almost won.

Don't quit when the hill is steepest,
For your goal is almost nigh;
Don't quit, for you're not a failure,
Until you fail to try!

~ Jill Wolf

CHAPTER 12
WHEN THE SPIRIT MOVES

When the Spirit of God moves, the winds of the soul are stirred and there is a beautiful atmosphere of praise! The Glory of the Lord comes down, people's lives are changed, and faith becomes visible by the working of miracles.

During the years we've lived in PNG, we have personally witnessed thousands receive the baptism of the Holy Ghost. The thrill of that Book of Acts experience can never be compared to any other. I beg to differ very strongly with those who do not believe that the Holy Spirit infilling is for us today. We have seen it happen, and cannot, nor do we wish to, deny it! It *is* for us today, and oh, what a joyous difference it makes in a person's life!

The late Rev. Billy Cole was a great evangelist who also had missions at the very core of his ministry. His love for anyone and everyone, has been felt the world over. He began to hold crusades in PNG in the early '90s.

Many have asked us about the retention rate of those thousands receiving the baptism of the Holy Ghost in our crusades, and we must confess, that it is not as high as we would like. One of the situations we face is the lack of pastors to teach the new converts. There is no doubt that the masses do indeed receive the Holy Spirit, but many of them simply go back to their original churches. You may argue with me at this point when I say that this is not necessarily bad. Sometimes these newly filled converts go back to their denominational churches, and end up converting their pastors and congregations.

Today in PNG, our average pastor has had only three months of training. There are several who have only been in the church one year, who are looking after new works. There are new churches springing up so rapidly in some areas that we cannot keep up with them all. If we could properly train a larger number of men and women to go out into the field, our churches would be able to handle the huge influx of new souls. That's why a proper training facility is so very important!!

However, we must not become frustrated. This is God's church, and He will take care of it. So often we'd love to hold on to the reins, but if the Lord is doing a work, why stop Him?

* * * *

In May of 1995, we traveled to a little village called *Giu,* deep in the highland mountains. We had church under a grass roof, with kerosene lanterns for light. The floor of the church was dirt and they had thrown dried grass all over it, for sitting on. The only way I can describe it, is that it was very much like having an old-fashioned church service in a small barn, with no electricity, and walls of bamboo instead of wood.

Brian had prepared a message, but felt that the Lord was directing him in a different direction. He felt impressed to speak to, and about, children. He couldn't get away from it. Finally, when the time came for him to preach, he discarded his notes and spoke very simply to the children.

When he was finished, he asked all of the children who needed the Holy Ghost to stand and come forward. There were at least 25 that came, of all ages.

He told them that even as a child they needed to repent for all their wrong doings, because that was part of God's plan that *everyone* needed to follow. Brian began to pray. The children began to lift their hands and repent, and cry out to God. Within just a couple of minutes, the Spirit of God began to fall and they began to speak in tongues! Some fell to the floor and wept, groaning and travailing in their new Spirit-filled language!

I couldn't help but get off my seat and get in close, because the Spirit of God was so strong. I felt like laughing and crying all at the same time.

Their prayers went up before the throne of God for quite some time, and we just enjoyed it! When all was said and done, we counted 19 of those children that had, beyond a shadow of a doubt, received the Holy Ghost!

If all dirt floors and bamboo churches were to produce this kind of humility and ready acceptance, let it be so everywhere!

* * * *

We are looking forward to continued revivals, no matter what! Indeed, there are challenges along the way, but anything worth having, is worth sacrificing for. If Jesus is nudging your heart to become involved in missions, you need to yield to Him no matter the cost. The rewards cannot be measured here on earth.

This world that we are living in is hungry and desperate for a genuine move of God. The Lord is searching for a people who will be fully committed to Him and His cause. Sure there are sacrifices, but what sacrifice can compare with Calvary? Indeed, with great sacrifice comes the promise of great reward!

More than anything, we must be Kingdom-minded, have our eyes set on Heaven, and take as many as we can with us!

Part of a crowd during one of our annual crusades.

A woman being filled with the baptism of the Holy Spirit

EPILOGUE

One of the most exciting and awesome events to attend in Papua New Guinea takes place every year at their Independence Day celebrations. These events are held around September 16, and tourists from all over the world come to see the spectacle. Every province and town has a celebration of some sort. They dress up in their tribal finery, dance their hearts out and beat their drums. We have witnessed several of these "sing sings" while here in PNG, and have taken many photos!

It's really awesome, and somewhat frightening, to be among thousands of dancers dressed in their traditional "bilas" (clothing/decorations), as they beat their drums and chant. The ground literally shakes under your feet.

Yet even more awesome, is to see these same people, whose lives have been changed by the power of Jesus Christ, dance before Him! No longer dancing, chanting, and beating their drums to honor dead ancestors, they now worship a living God who is closer to them than a brother!

Tribal Dancers beating their drums and chanting.

Esther surrounded by Asaro villagers, discussing the power of their homemade bows and arrows.

RECIPES

Tomato Soup - PNG Style
Yield: 4 Servings

Great appetizer or light lunch!

6 Tomatoes, large and ripe	2 Medium Carrots, diced
1 - 1 1/2 Cup Coconut Milk (whole milk can be substituted)	2 Cloves Garlic, minced
2 Green Onions, or 1 Leek, finely chopped	1 Teaspoon Ginger, grated
1 Medium Sweet Potato, diced	Salt and Pepper, to taste

Chop tomatoes into small chunks (Do NOT peel nor seed them) In large pan on medium heat, combine tomatoes and potato. Cook until tomatoes are "juiced", then add remaining ingredients. Turn down heat and simmer for about 20 minutes, stirring occasionally.

Note: I use all fresh ingredients and chop them in a food processor.

Pancakes - PNG Style

Flame Flour (Wholemeal) - PNG

1 Cup Flour (whole-wheat)   Pinch Salt
1 Egg   1 1/4 Cup Milk

Place all ingredients into a bowl and beat with a wooden spoon or hand rotary beater until smooth. Heat a medium size frying pan or griddle, grease lightly with butter and using 8 tbsp batter for each pancake, pour into hot pan and cook slowly until bubbles appear on surface.

Turn pancake over and cook until golden brown. Place onto serving plate, sprinkle with sugar and lemon juice, roll up and serve.

* * * *

Pumpkin Soup
Yield: 6 Servings

From the kitchens of New Zealand/Australia - This one is my favorite!

2 Lbs (750g) Pumpkin, peeled and chopped   To Taste:
1 Large Potato, chopped   Salt
1 Onion, chopped   Black Pepper
4 Cups Chicken Stock   Nutmeg

Put pumpkin, potato and onion into a large saucepan. Add stock. Cover, bring to boiling and cook until vegetables are soft. In blender, puree the soup (or push through a sieve). Season with spices to taste. Serve Hot.

For extra flavor, add ham hock or bacon when cooking pumpkin.

Peanut Stew

Boral Gas Co., PNG

1 Onion, or a few Shallots
2 Tablespoon Oil
1 Cup Raw Peanuts, shelled
1 Sweet Potato, cooked
1 Large Taro Root, cooked (you could substitute regular potato)

Tomatoes, cooked
Carrots, cooked
Fresh Ginger, grated
Coconut Milk

Heat oil in fry pan, with grated fresh ginger. Stir in cooked veggies and potatoes.

Squeeze in coconut milk and stir. Add peanuts and stir-fry for a few minutes. Season with salt and if necessary, add a little water if it is too dry. Simmer over low heat for 15 minutes. Serve hot.

Mock Teriyaki Chicken
Yield: 3 Servings

Barbara Kisekol, a Papua New Guinean, spent 2 years with a missionary family in the Yukon, as she went to school there. The lady of the house taught her some "tricks of the trade" when it came to "western" cooking. This is one that Barbara taught to me! This is awesome meat when served with rice, tossed salad and iced tea!

1 Whole Frying Chicken, (or chicken pieces - wings work great)
1 Cup Water
1/2 Cup Kikkoman Soy Sauce*

1 Tablespoon Butter

Pinch Salt

*NOTE: another brand soy sauce can be substituted, however, the flavor will not be as close to a teriyaki flavor.

Bring all ingredients except chicken to a boil. Cut chicken into 8 pieces, and add to boiling stock. Cover and simmer, turning often, for 1/2 hour or until chicken is done.

Meatballs

Flame Flour (PNG)

2 Cup Hamburger, or canned Corned Beef

1 Cup Flour

1 Egg, beaten

1/2 Cup Water or Milk

1/2 Tablespoon Salt, (and some curry, optional)

2 Teaspoons Baking Powder

Combine all ingredients, shape into small balls and fry in hot oil.

Serving Suggestions: Serve with rice, *kaukau* (sweet potato) banana or vegetable.

Highland Fish Soup
Yield: 6 Servings

From Trukai Rice (PNG)

1 Tablespoon Butter	2 Cups Tuna, Cooked Or Heated
1 Onion, Medium and Chopped	1 Cup Natural Brown Rice, uncooked
1 Tablespoon Flour	Parsley, Finely Chopped
425 grams (13 Oz) Canned Tomatoes	4 Chicken Bouillon Cubes

Cook brown rice using rapid boil method (see below for details) Dissolve bouillon cubes into 2 cups hot water. Heat butter in large saucepan and lightly fry onion. Blend in flour then gradually stir in chicken stock. Stir until smooth. Add tomatoes, fish and cooked rice. Simmer for approx. 10 minutes. Sprinkle with fresh parsley and serve.

RAPID BOIL METHOD:
Bring 4 cups water to a boil.
Stir in 1 cup of natural brown rice and salt to taste.
Return to a boil and simmer gently uncovered for 25-30 minutes. Drain into strainer.

Homemade Shake-N-Fry Mix
Yield: 3 Cups

This is another of my own creations. I was desperate for a nice Shake-N-Fry (or Shake-N-Bake), but no such luck in Papua New Guinea! So I began to experiment with flour and breadcrumbs as my base, and different spices. I tried several different variations, and one day my husband said, "This is it! You better write it down right now, before you forget!" So I did...and now I share it with you. This Shake-N-Fry (or Bake) is all we ever use anymore! It really is delicious, and makes an excellent cold picnic chicken, too!

3 Cups Flour, or 1-1/2 cups Flour and 1-1/2 cups of breadcrumbs
2 Tablespoon Chicken Seasoning (I use Tones® Montreal Chicken Seasoning)
1/8 Cup Salt
2 Teaspoon Curry Powder
1 Teaspoon White Pepper
1 Tablespoon Parsley or dried celery leaves

1/2 Teaspoon Each:
Cumin
Marjoram
Oregano
Rosemary
Cayenne
Paprika
Sage
Thyme
Onion Powder

Mix all ingredients into a large plastic Ziploc bag. When ready to coat meat, wash meat and pat dry, then put the meat pieces into the bag and shake! Immediately remove meat and fry. Mix can be used again and again, until it is finished.

Note: Be sure to seal Ziploc and store mix in the refrigerator after initial use.

BAKED CHICKEN BREASTS
(using the *Homemade Shake-N-Fry* Recipe):

Preheat oven to 350° F (180° C).

Coat chicken with Homemade Shake-N-Fry.

Arrange chicken in a single layer in a greased, ovenproof baking dish.

Bake for 10 minutes, turning the chicken over and baking for 10 minutes more.

Baking times may vary depending on the size of your chicken pieces and whether or not they contain bones.

(This recipe reflects baking with boneless, skinless, flattened chicken breasts.)

* * * *

Homemade Peanut Butter
Bima Dege (Papua New Guinea)

Peanuts, slightly roasted and salted
Oil

Remove the skins of the roasted peanuts. Fry peanuts in a frying pan with a little oil. Smash the peanuts until they are close to a "dust" consistency. (Blenders will help this process). Put the peanut "dust" into a jar. Mix in just enough oil to disperse throughout the peanut dust. Let it sit until it becomes soft, the consistency of peanut butter. Add more oil if necessary.

Creamy Custard Rice
Yield: 7 Servings

Turkai Rice (PNG): Serve either hot or cold.

1/2 Cup Rice, uncooked	1 Teaspoon Salt
1/2 Cup Dry Milk	1 Tablespoon Custard Powder
1/4 Cup Sugar	1/2 Cup Raisins

Cook rice. Blend milk powder with 1-1/2 cups water. Add 1-1/4 cups of milk and sugar to the rice. Bring to a boil and simmer for 3 minutes. Mix custard powder with remaining 1/4 cup milk in large bowl to form a paste. Mix raisins into rice then pour into the custard mixture (off stove) and stir well. Return combined mixture to saucepan, bring to boil and stir until thoroughly blended.

* * * *

Creamy Peanut Chicken
Yield: 4 Servings

Trukai Rice (PNG): This flavor is the most unusual combination. It may seem like something you wouldn't want to try, but believe me, it's very rich, filling, and delicious!

1 ½ Cups Rice, uncooked	1 Tablespoon Raw Sugar
2 Tablespoons Curry Powder	1 Tablespoon Oyster Sauce (or any fish sauce)
1 lb (500 G) Boneless Chicken Breasts, cut into strips	1/2 Cup Crunchy Peanut Butter
1 Tablespoon Olive Oil	
1 Cup Coconut Milk, (or use whole milk)	

Cook rice using absorption method. Blend curry powder with water to form a paste. Blend paste with chicken. Heat oil in pan, add chicken mixture and fry for 5 minutes or until golden brown. Blend coconut milk powder with 2 cups warm water. Add remaining ingredients and bring to a boil. Lower heat and simmer for 10 minutes or until sauce has thickened. Serve over cooked rice.

* * * *

Baked Sago With Over Ripe Bananas

Boral Gas, PNG

1 Cup Sago	Aluminum Foil, (or Banana Leaves)
2 Coconuts	
8-10 Bananas, over ripe	

Dry sago and strain.

Mash over-ripe bananas and mix with sago. Place the mixed sago in aluminum foil or banana leaf, then sprinkle the scraped coconut on top. Close and secure foil or leaf.

Bake at 180°C (350°F) for 30-40 minutes.

Squeeze scraped coconut (no water added) and collect the milk.

Pour coconut milk in pan and bring to simmer until thick. Spoon coconut cream over baked sago when serving.

Aibika Rice Bake
Yield: 6 Servings

1 Bunch Aibika (can be substituted with Chinese Cabbage), finely chopped
1 Tablespoon Worcestershire
1 Small Onion, finely chopped
3 Cups Cheese, grated

1 Cup Rice, Uncooked
4 Eggs
1/4 Cup Butter, Melted
1/3 Cup Dry Milk
Salt To Taste

Cook rice using the absorption method. Blend milk powder with one cup of water. Cook and drain aibika.

Beat eggs, then add milk, onion, 2 cups cheese, salt and Worcestershire. Add to a greased ovenproof baking dish. Fold in cooked aibika, rice and butter. Sprinkle remaining cheese on top and bake at 190° C (375° F) for 30 minutes.

Rice Cereal (Hot)
Yield: 4 Servings

My own creation, made out of necessity! In PNG we eat lots of rice, and invariably have leftovers. This recipe is a real treat on cool mornings and the leftover rice isn't wasted! :)

4 or 5 Cups cooked or leftover Rice
1 Teaspoon Salt
500 ml (2 ¼ Cups) Milk
1 Tablespoon Cinnamon
1/3 Cup Brown Sugar
1 Tablespoon Butter
Raisins, optional

In a large saucepan, combine all ingredients except raisins. Heat on med-low heat until everything is quite hot, and the rice has absorbed some of the milk. The consistency should be creamy, and not "doughy" - add more milk if necessary.

Remove raisin cereal from the heat and stir in a handful of raisins before serving. Makes generous portions, and will warm the heart as well!

Strawberry Yogurt Drink
Yield: 6 Servings

This is my own creation, borne out of necessity to use up the very ripened strawberries before they went bad! This recipe is excellent if frozen in small portions (such as an ice cube tray) and blended once again when frozen. Talk about an excellent, refreshing summer drink!!

3 Cups Strawberries, very ripe
3 Cups Pineapple Juice
3 Cups Yogurt, (I used Soy Yogurt)
4 Tablespoons Honey, (I used whipped honey)

Blend all ingredients together in a blender on medium speed until thoroughly blended.

Drink immediately or freeze in small portions and blend it later while it's frozen, to make summer slush!

ORDERING:

You may order paperback copies of this book by sending $15 USD each via PayPal to <u>BookSales.Nali@gmail.com</u>, along with the following information:

1. Your mailing address;
2. How many copies you are requesting, and
3. Whether you want the book(s) signed by the author.

Made in the USA
Columbia, SC
04 April 2023